The 1980 Pere Marquette
Theology Lecture

METHOD
IN
THEOLOGY:
AN ORGANON
FOR OUR TIME

by
FREDERICK. E. CROWE, S.J.
Research Professor in Theology
Regis College, Toronto

Marquette University Press
Milwaukee, Wisconsin 53233

Library of Congress Catalog Number 80-81015
ISBN 0-87462-519-X

No one, so far as I know, has ever done for Theology what Bacon did for physical science, and since I saw the announcement of your Essay I have been looking for its appearance with great curiosity and interest, for there are many passages in your writings which indicate that you had given very much thought to many of the questions which would be illustrated in a Theological *Novum Organum*.

Robert William Dale, to John Henry Newman, March 13, 1870 in Vol. 25 of *The Letters and Diaries of John Henry Newman,* ed. Charles S. Dessain (Oxford: Clarendon Press, 1973) p. 56.

You have truly said that we need a Novum Organum for theology—and I shall be truly glad if I shall be found to have made any suggestions which will aid the formation of such a calculus—but it must be the strong conception and the one work of a great genius, not the obiter attempt of a person like myself, who has already attempted many things, and is at the end of his days.

John Henry Newman in reply, March 16, 1970, *ibid.,* pp. 56-57.

METHOD IN THEOLOGY:

An Organon For Our Time

The Pere Marquette Lecture has this year a somewhat particular purpose, deriving from the fact that Fr. Bernard Lonergan has just completed three-quarters of a century of life. There are family ways of celebrating such an event, but the academic world has its ways too; for that world is not so inhumanly academic as to ignore the milestones in the lives of its leaders, or to fail to celebrate those milestones with its own modest pomp and appropriate ceremonies. And so, joining friends of Fr. Lonergan around the world, we offer this lecture to honor one who has deserved well of the world of learning, in its secular as well as its religious branches, to express our gratitude for the notable benefits he has brought to the fields of theology, philosophy, and the range of sciences, both natural and human, and not omitting to ask ourselves what might be a suitable re-

sponse to and continuation of the work he
has initiated.

For my own part the year's celebrations
have given me an occasion and a stimulus
to reflect at length on the whole Lonergan
enterprise (the course of the lecture will
explain my choice of that phrase), and so
I thought I could best use the opportunity
afforded me if, instead of listing and prais-
ing Fr. Lonergan's achievements in academe, I were to make a new effort to
understand what he has been about during most of these seventy-five years, and
to clarify for ourselves the tasks to which
his contribution challenges us. Note that
the key words are "understanding" and
"challenge." Surely "understanding" has
been utterly central to his enterprise, so
what is more appropriate as a way of
honoring him than the effort to understand
what he is doing himself? "Challenge," on
the other hand, is not the word he regu-
larly uses to describe the effective thrust
of his work; he prefers to speak of an "in-
vitation." But what he issues as an invita-
tion we must receive as a challenge; his

famous fourth level of intentionality, the existential side of academe, has taught us that much. And so we cannot rest content with a personally satisfying, but ultimately selfish, effort to understand; we must be ready also to respond, that is, to take up "responsibly" the tasks his work has set for us.

I speak of a "new" effort to grasp the significance of Lonergan's contribution, and I thereby acknowledge the efforts that have already been made, starting thirty years ago and increasing sharply in volume during the last decade, to study, understand, locate in history, and evaluate the elusive and difficult, but fundamental and momentous thought of this scientist-humanist-philosopher-theologian. I cannot take account here of those previous efforts; I can only declare the help they have been to me in my own long and groping search. But I think something different from what they have provided is called for on the present occasion. And perhaps too it is possible now, at any rate appropriate to make the attempt, to see beyond studies of this or that particular idea and to grasp the pattern of his lifework as a whole; going beyond that even, to anticipate the direction of his influence on history. Not as if his work were over, but after seventy-five years one expects, especially in such a long-range thinker as Lonergan is, to see a pattern. And not as if we intended to stop the pattern here either; there might yet be the introduction of an innovative element. But we do not expect any radical reversal of direction or violent disturbance of the pattern; when such an intellectual architect builds, he builds well and on secure foundations. So it seems feasible to attempt now a view of his lifework as a whole, and of the enterprise to which he has given momentum.

A simple and helpful way to begin is that of comparison with other thinkers on the contemporary scene. But we will surely wish, all of us, to avoid the failings to which such comparisons are prone; and so our procedure will be a matter of noticing different approaches, different needs envisaged, different contributions to meet them, something in fact like different vocations. I have in mind especially that group of Roman Catholic philosophers and theologians who, before, during, and after the Second Vatican Council were so powerful a factor for our *aggiornamento*, pointing us into the modern world and helping us endure the "growing pains" of that traumatic transition. Before the Council they were raising the questions long suppressed by our attachment to continuity (and getting their knuckles rapped for it too); during the Council they were, it is said, the teachers of the bishops; and after the Council they embarked on such promising ventures as *Concilium* (later balanced by *Communio*) to continue the good work begun. They are, I think it is fair to say, and I say it with profound respect, the "now" theologians. By this I mean that they are deeply concerned to meet the needs of God's people in an updated theology, and to do it, as far as possible, here and now when the needs are acutely felt; they are doing so with erudition, intelligence, and notable wisdom (I do not deny there are exceptions!), and doing so in every field, not only in traditional areas of theology but in the many areas in which new data as well as a new concept of science, a new sense of history, and a new philosophy are raising ever new questions for the theologians.

We need these philosophers and theologians, and we need them now. I wish with all sincerity to pay them honor and to acknowledge our common debt to their industry and intelligence. But I think it is quite misleading to classify Lonergan, as is often done, in the same group with them. His way is different. We might grasp the difference by asking whether the "now" theologians are also the theologians of the future: is their work destined mainly to tide us over present difficulties, to provide some sort of light in present darkness, or will it endure, a beacon for generations and maybe centuries? I am not a prophet in these matters, and, though I have my opinion, neither I nor anyone else can be dogmatic on the question; we must leave it to the long pondering of history to decide with authority. But the question at least reveals the possibility of a different way. There may be other needs for theologians to meet (or perhaps one will say in the end another analysis of the fundamental need). These other needs must be met by other theologians taking a different approach and producing quite different work. Their way will be deliberately to set aside the provision of immediate relief for present needs, to aim at a more distant target, and to move with all their energies toward that goal, in the hope at least of leaving the legacy of a direction and a momentum for others to attain it. This, I think, is what Lonergan has been about. He is not a "now" theologian. He has made it his task to build for the future; his concern has been the long-range concern; he looks to a complete restructuring of theology as the answer to our most fundamental need; and his energies have been devoted consistently toward attaining that goal, however distant it still remains.

We are dealing, then, in a true sense, with quite different vocations. There is no need to evaluate them in terms of merit. How would one compare a Mother Teresa zealously feeding the hungry with an equally zealous agronomist working for the increase of the world's food supply? But what is important is to notice the different need that preoccupies a thinker like Lonergan. His analysis of our situation involves a quite specific view of history and of the magnitude of the transition through which the human race is now passing. Karl Jaspers has said: "For more than a hundred years it has been gradually realized that the history of scores of centuries is drawing to a close."[1] The idea is startling enough even at first glance; it becomes staggering as its real meaning dawns on us. I do not know whether Lonergan has read this particular phrase in Jaspers, but he has worked most of his life as if his purpose had been guided by that thought, as if a great new era were opening before us, as if we were going through a transition unparallelled, not just in centuries but in millennia, with a consequent need not just to rethink the old questions in philosophy and theology and add the new ones, but to rebuild from the ground up, to restructure completely the whole edifice.

I have been trying to characterize the general thrust of Lonergan's lifework, and have been doing so by way of contrast with the aims and objectives, the vocation and strategy, the orientation and approach, of contemporary thinkers. But we need a more positive characterization, a more specific indication, and I have a simple clue to guide us. We have built up, in our Lonergan Research Center at Regis College, a card index of secondary literature, with a subdivision for topics explored. You will find listed there studies of Lonergan's views on Abstraction, Affirmation, Art, and so on, right down to Wisdom, World, and Zoology. But you will also find a small subdivision under the heading, "Lonergan Applied," with a rather odd series of such applications: Architecture, Canon Law, Catholic Education, Cultures of Canada, Feminism, Mathematics, Politi-

cal Science, Psychotherapy, University
Students, and so on. There is a clue here,
and more than a clue, to Lonergan's specific contribution to the intellectual enterprise, enabling us to recognize a fact quite
central for assessing his thought and locating him in history. Namely, that whatever else his lifework may be, however
penetrating his analyses and however im-
pressive his ideas, his thought is ultimately
oriented to the practical, it is programmatic for the future. That is, he has provided us with an instrument that is to be
used, not just contemplated, and the real
Lonergan of history is not so much the
Lonergan studied and analyzed, discussed
and debated, located and evaluated, but
the Lonergan who is still to be applied to
the urgent tasks of the new age that we
are facing.

I believe that this understanding of
Lonergan will enable us to structure his
lifework as a unity, to characterize it in its
overall thrust and momentum and impact.
At any rate it will determine the direction
and divisions of this lecture, in which I

present Lonergan's contribution as a new
organon for our times. "New" organon
suggests some relation to older forms, and
that corresponds exactly to my purpose.
There are antecedents for the creation of
an organon, and I will turn to them for
illumination. At certain momentous points
in history, this Greek word or its equiva-
lent has been used to designate an instrument of mind: not an instrument of the
hand, like a hammer or nutmeg-grater, or
even so precious an instrument as a Stradi-
varius violin, but rather a mentality, a
formation of incarnate spirit, a way of
structuring our conscious activities, that
has been of immense importance for the
ongoing work of the human race. Such
was the case with the Aristotelian organon,
the logic of twenty-three hundred years
ago, and such was the case again not quite
four hundred years ago with the *novum
organum* for experimental science of
Francis Bacon. In this lecture I propose to
look at these two instances in their relation
to Lonergan, not with the suggestion that
they were direct influences and sources

determining his lifework, but as notions
which we may abstract from history for
the clarification of his thought and purpose. To speak of abstracting the notions
from history is my way of admitting that
I cannot treat Aristotle or Bacon with the
detail and scholarship that experts in their
thought would demand. But all the same
I think we can learn a great deal even from
an amateur's approach. This lecture, then,
has four parts: first, Aristotle and the organon that he unwittingly but in fact cre-
ated; then, Bacon and the consciously conceived notion of an organon; thirdly, Lonergan's lifework as that of creating a fundamental method; and, fourthly, that
method conceived as an organon in a series
with the Aristotelian and Baconian forms.

I. Aristotle and the Creation of
an Organon

Aristotle's main use of the term, organon,
was biological;[2] and that is still the central usage today: heart and lungs are
organs in the sense that they are parts of
the body, each with its differentiated struc-

ture and specific function, each serving
the life of the body as a whole. There is a
secondary use in Aristotle: the word, organon, is applied to means of investigation. He conceived investigation in terms
of the hunt for game; but, instead of or-
dinary weapons (bows and arrows, I suppose, and nets and spears), the intellectual
hunt uses propositions, choosing them, dis-
tinguishing their meanings, comparing
them, etc.[3]

If it is the biological use of organon
that suggests the enduring and substantive
character of the method we have under-
taken to study, and I will later invoke the
biological use for that purpose, still it is
Aristotle's secondary use that is most directly related to our topic. Now Aristotle
himself never referred to his logical works,
or even to the apparatus of logic in general, as an organon; that was left to his followers several centuries later, though they
merely took the step that was implicit in
the master's attitude. For logic is in fact
an organon and so did not enter Aristotle's
division of the sciences. He saw them as

three in number: "the theoretical, the practical, and the productive." Logic does not belong to any of the three; it is "a part of general culture which everyone should undergo before he studies any science." That is Ross's view, and he informs us also that this attitude "underlies the application of the word *Organon* or *instrument* (sc. of science) to logical doctrine and ultimately to the collection of Aristotle's logical works."[4]

Let us turn, then, to that application and to the eloquent plea made by Alexander of Aphrodisias, five centuries after Aristotle, for the study of logic: ". . . logic is not less deserving of our attention and study owing to the fact that it is an instrument of philosophy rather than an actual part of philosophy:"[5] Why? Because our greatest good is to become like God, this likeness is achieved through knowledge, and knowledge in turn is gained through demonstration in logic. Later still by three more centuries, that is, only in the sixth century of our era, the term, *Organon,* came to be applied to the collection of Aristotle's logical works.[6] This logical corpus was translated into Latin in the early part of the middle ages, and thus became a powerful tool and beneficent influence operative in western culture right into our own day.

What emerges from this little exercise in armchair history? Without becoming experts in the Categories, the book On Interpretation, the books on the Prior and Posterior Analytics, and the rest, and relying mainly on that common notion of traditional Aristotelian logic which has entered rather deeply into our culture, we have, I think, enough data to form a preliminary notion of an organon understood as an instrument of mind. One writer suggests "that the Aristotelian contribution is, not so much any doctrine or body of doctrine, as a contribution to the stuff of thought itself." And he observes that, whereas we have in common use terms like "Hegelianism" and "Platonism," we have "no analogous Aristotelianism."[7] I cannot say whether Aristotelians would agree to all that, just as I cannot say whether philoso-

phers have a consensus on locating logic
outside the main body of philosophical
thought. But at least we have the notion,
in a fairly clear and simple instance, of an
instrument of mind that serves the intellectual quest as bows and arrows serve
the hunter's task. And just as it will profit
the hunter in the long run to leave the
hunt and make a better bow and arrow,
so one expects that to set aside for a time
the direct pursuit of knowledge in a given
field, in order to create a better instrument of investigation, cannot but profit
the thinker, and enormously expedite the
advance of learning in the long run of intellectual progress. If there remains an
ambiguity and a debate over the place of
logic within the very corpus of philosophy,
well, that too is relevant to our appropriation of this Aristotelian notion, for it
has been disputed also about Lonergan's
thought whether it is to be conceived as
a theory and system or as a way—a good
question, but one I do not need to settle
in this lecture.

II. *Bacon and the* Novum Organum

Whereas Aristotle had to wait nearly a thousand years for his logical corpus to be designated an organon of philosophy, Francis Bacon was in more of a hurry. He himself appropriated the Latin form of the term for his purpose, speaking of a *Novum Organum,* and doing so in direct contrast to the old *organum* that derived from Aristotle. Aristotle, at least as the Schoolmen were promoting him, was one great enemy of the true advancement of learning. He and his Schoolmen followers "embody the common fallacies of the *sophistical* or *rationalistic* school." Too impatient to form general concepts and axioms by abstraction from particulars, they do not attend enough to experience and the facts. "They use logical categories not to clarify experience but to force it into preconceived molds. Deductive reasoning predominates, while the experimental study of nature is kept at a minimum."[8]

What was one to do in this sorry but widely prevalent situation? Bacon, rather a pessimist on human intelligence, had no hope that the reigning errors would be corrected "either by the natural force of the understanding or by help of the aids and instruments of Logic." So he came to his own positive program: "There was but one course left, therefore—to try the whole thing anew upon a better plan, and to commence a total reconstruction of sciences, arts, and all human knowledge, raised upon the proper foundations."[9] The general direction of Bacon's "better plan" is well known: as Collins says, the form of reasoning "must be transformed from a primarily deductive one to an inductive one."[10] The details are more complicated, and must be omitted here.

What I think we can gain by a selective reading of Bacon is a new clarity on the very idea of an organon, and on the role in the intellectual community of one who conceives his lifework as that of creating such an instrument. Here Bacon takes us beyond Aristotle. For Bacon had a very explicit self-understanding in regard to his role in the world of learning, and considered his work to be programmatic in the highest degree. He was bent on a "Magna Instauratio" of knowledge.[11] The translators give us "The Great Instauration" for this Latin phrase; can we not ask them to do better? The Greek root of the word, *stauros,* means post (you remember that the New Testament uses this word for the cross), and the image of an *instauratio* is that of bringing back to its upright position a post that has begun to lean dangerously toward the ground. But that too is rather pedestrian; what Bacon has in mind is more like another renaissance in its scope, the rebuilding of the temple of learning, the restoration of academe, the renewal of the intellectual life in the measure in which the Second Vatican Council was to be a renewal of the church.

Further, he conceives his own part as that of creating the instrument of this renewal, the *novum organum.* The old one, logic, had failed, and so "the entire work of the understanding [must] be commenced afresh, and the mind itself be

from the very outset not left to take its
own course, but guided at every step; and
the business be done as if by machinery."
He argues that we do not work with our
naked hands in mechanical matters but
use tools to do the job; similarly, we
should not work in intellectual matters
"with little else than the naked forces of
the understanding," but should construct
tools for the purpose,[12] what he a little
later calls "instruments of the mind."[13]
And, lastly, he conceives his part to have
been mainly that of showing the way, and
offering hope of better things in the future; he asks us to "consider what may be
expected (after the way has been thus
indicated) from men abounding in leisure,
and from association of labours, and from
successions of ages."[14] He himself cannot
"hope to live to complete . . . the Instauration . . . but," he says, I "hold it enough
if in the intermediate business I bear myself soberly and profitably, sowing in the
meantime for future ages the seeds of
a purer truth, and performing my part

towards the commencement of the great undertaking."[15]

I have to resist the temptation here to run ahead of my topic and to draw comparisons between Bacon and Lonergan: contrasts surely, for Lonergan would hardly speak of guiding the mind "as if by machinery"; but broad similarities too in the idea and scope of the enterprise. My purpose, however, is not really to compare Bacon and Lonergan; I leave that project to some aspiring student in search of a dissertation topic. It is rather to form from a historical instance, somewhat abstractly considered, a clearer notion of what an organon is and of the relation in which its creator stands to the ongoing tasks of science. And here Bacon is especially illuminating: he did not see his contribution to lie in the investigations he himself carried on, though they always interested him (in fact, indulgence of his scientific curiosity on a certain cold day led to bronchitis and his ensuing death), but as providing an organon and a method. He recognized the need the human mind has to stand back from the particular task, and to discover the proper and effective way to knowledge.

Some of his commentators underline this feature of his work. Jones says of him that "his influence on the scientific movement was general rather than specific."[16] And Whitaker, that he "had the wisdom to concentrate on surveying the state of knowledge in preference to surveying knowledge," and that he "saw the importance of methodology as none of the encyclopedists did";[17] he could not, Whitaker continues, chart the way to advancement of learning, but "he could call upon men to attempt the journey and show how it began."[18]

III. Lonergan's Lifework: Creating a Fundamental Method

These two little forays into history have been extremely illuminating for me in studying the lifework of Lonergan. The organon which Aristotle's disciples made of their master's logic, and the way Bacon saw his role in the advancement of science, have helped me personally to conceive more clearly what Lonergan has been doing throughout his career, and to understand how the strategy he has mapped out leaves the whole theological campaign still to be conducted by later generations. For he too, like Bacon, has very clearly seen that the need of the times is not so much for a new set of answers to the problems of the day, as it is for a whole new beginning. He speaks of the movement in this century "towards a total transformation of dogmatic theology,"[19] and himself calls for "a complete restructuring of Catholic theology,"[20] in phrases that are a remarkable echo of Bacon's purpose "to commence a total reconstruction of sciences, arts, and all human knowledge, raised upon the proper foundations."[21]

So it was that for thirty-four years, from the start of his doctoral dissertation in 1938 till the publication of his *Method in Theology* in 1972, he labored to create the instrument of mind, in Bacon's terms, or instrument of incarnate spirit, in terms more congenial to his own thought, that

would do the job. It is, of course, utterly
impossible in this lecture to follow the
course of his thinking throughout those
years: the particular ideas that he formed,
the general plans he conceived, the ex-
pansion, correction, revision of his methodology, its tentative application and subsequent transposition to higher viewpoints.
Research has only begun on the history
of his thought, and there remain vast
stretches of *terra incognita*. But I do think
it will be helpful to select two rather key
points in the earlier stages of his development and set them in contrast to the relatively finished product he has given us in
Method.

The first is the now almost famous Introduction to his doctoral dissertation on
the Thomist concept of operative grace. I
say "almost famous," for Lonergan never
published this Introduction, even though
the body of his dissertation went into print
in 1941-1942 and again in 1971.[22] But few
unpublished pages from a dissertation
have been so often referred to, or been in
such demand on the black market of the-

ological xeroxing. The urgent need, as
Lonergan saw it in this Introduction, was
for some guiding method. And he saw the
need, as Bacon had seen it, simply by ob-
serving the sad state of theology as it ex-
isted, especially in the theology of grace
where Dominican-Jesuit controversies had
for three long centuries manifested the
bitter symptoms of decline. Lonergan's
own work was to be a historical study of
Thomas Aquinas, and he did not expect
more from historical study than probability; but if that probability was to be, instead of an opinion, a scientific conclusion,
he felt that some method tending to
greater objectivity than those employed
through three centuries had to be found.
Now where does one look for a method
to guide the mind? Well, there have been
some startling advances in the natural sciences, and Lonergan finds a clue there.
He continues:

> The quantitative sciences are objective sim-
> ply because they are given by mathematics an
> *a priori* scheme of such generality that there
> can be no tendency to do violence to the data

for the sake of maintaining the scheme. But the same benefit is obtained for the history of speculative theology by an analysis of the idea of its development, for the analysis does yield a general scheme but it does so . . . solely from a consideration of the nature of human speculation on a given subject.[23]

What Lonergan is seeking here, as he puts it himself, "is a point of vantage outside the temporal dialectic, a matrix or system of thought that at once is as pertinent and as indifferent to historical events as is the science of mathematics to quantitative phenomena."[24] And this vantage point he finds in the nature of human speculation, in a scheme that is not merely hypothetical but demonstrable, and this "because the human mind is always the human mind."[25] On this basis he draws up, in what we might call his earliest transcendental deduction, the seven phases of unfolding dialectic that will plot the course of any theological question that develops specific and generic theorems. And he verifies the seven phases in "the speculative movement from St. Augustine's *De Cor-*

reptione et Gratia to the *Prima Secundae* of St. Thomas."[26]

This is heady stuff, perhaps the sort of thing one might expect from a brilliant theologian just at the beginning of his career. It is possible to see here anticipations of the great work of 1972: the young Lonergan is already in search of a "matrix or system of thought" that would stand outside of and be a guide for actual theology, and already he is trying to formulate it in terms of the invariant operations of the mind. But perhaps it is also possible to discover here the distance the young Lonergan has still to go for his definitive method. He obviously was himself well enough aware of the limitations of his idea, since he never offered it to the public in print. In any case, it was designed to guide only a part of theology, the investigation of a speculative development, and Lonergan had still to discover, accept, and integrate into his method the ranges of theology that do not fall under that heading.

One measure of the magnitude of the task he had set himself is the time that intervened before his next formulation of theological method, and the extent of the preliminary studies he found it necessary to undertake in those intervening years. For the next real effort to conceive his method came off the drafting-board only in 1954, when the painstaking historical researches of the *verbum* articles had been completed,[27] and *Insight* was already in its final form if not yet accepted by a publisher.[28] The method is sketched in a review-article, "Theology and Understanding,"[29] in which Lonergan states his own acceptance of basic Thomist principles of theology and at the same time acknowledges "the existence of contemporary methodological issues that cannot be dispatched in so expeditious a fashion."[30] Thus, his method here is anchored firmly, as the earlier method was, in the concrete issues raised by historical figures, as well as in the testing-ground of actual theological treatises, this time in the two parts of his Trinitarian theology, published in 1957

and 1961,[31] but elaborated earlier in his
lectures at the theological schools of Mon-
treal, Toronto, and Rome.

At this time, Lonergan's notion of
method is dominated by the scheme of
the twofold order of thought, the analytic
and synthetic.[32] The analytic begins with
what is immediate, which in theology is
the gospel message, truths of faith distilled
from the revelation God made to his people. Analysis could be conceived to pro-
ceed atemporally, but only in some angelic
mind. For human theologians analysis
takes place historically, in the dialectic of
thinking and erring minds, with slow
formulation of the faith by the church,
with dead ends, stagnant stretches, and
the quantum leaps that history displays.
But its end-product, the goal toward which
it ever tends, the system to which it is still
subordinate in Lonergan's hierarchy of
theological values, is that fundamental understanding of the mysteries of faith which
is the synthetic view. Such a synthetic
view will begin with the basic concepts at
which analysis arrived and, proceeding in

exactly the reverse order, work back to the
immediate features of the gospel message
from which analysis had begun. We are
back then where we began, but back with
a difference, endowed with that most
fruitful understanding of which the First
Vatican Council spoke and which Lonergan still regards in 1954 as the proper
business of theology. "With some approximation to a single view," he writes, "it
gives rise to an apprehension of the exact
content and the exact implications of the
many mysteries in their many aspects.
That single view both simplifies and en-
riches one's own spiritual life and it be-
stows upon one's teaching the enviable
combination of sureness of doctrine with
versatility of expression."[33]

This brilliant scheme is by no means to
be written off as a mere stepping-stone to
a later successful idea. I think, in fact, that
Method in Theology will itself suffer if we
do not bring forward and incorporate into
it more of the content of the analytic-synthetic idea. And nevertheless the analytic-
synthetic scheme was not enough for the

task before him. First of all, historical process was attached rather awkwardly to the twofold movement. In the 1957 work of trinitarian theology, where this method is set forth more completely than in the article of 1954, we have the three movements described, but the twofold analytic-synthetic process seems by itself to constitute an integral way, which nevertheless has to be completed by a third, the historical.[34] Further, I have already mentioned Lonergan's advertence to contemporary factors that do not fit well in the Aristotelian and Thomist thinking at the basis of the twofold way. They are four: the *Denkformen*, later to be elaborated in the patterns of consciousness and stages of meaning; the relation between speculative and positive theology, later transformed in the context of the two phases of mediating and mediated theology; the relation between speculative theology and the empirical human sciences, later to be rethought on the basis of the first four chapters of *Method;* and the whole business of knowing what one's knowing is:

> For then the issues of historical interpretation
> are complicated by the self-knowledge of the
> interpreter, by his difficulty in grasping clearly
> and distinctly just what he is doing when he
> understands and conceives, reflects and judges.
> Nor is this difficulty to be overcome in any
> easy fashion, for it has all the complexity of
> the critical problem.[35]

And so it was back to the drafting-board
for a third try; it would be eighteen years
from the article, "Theology and Understanding," to the relatively definitive work
on method.[36]

These bits of history are quite inade-
quate to convey the Herculean effort of
thirty-four years that produced *Method in
Theology:* to speak of going to the drafting-board three times at intervals of sixteen and eighteen years gives little idea
of the courses, lectures, institutes, sets of
notes, and published materials that mark
the stages of the struggle. But perhaps I
have at least highlighted the fact that
Lonergan's great work was indeed the
end-product of a lifetime of thought. It is
on that work of a lifetime that his position
in history will stand or fall.[37]

As for *Method in Theology* itself, I can perhaps suppose some degree of familiarity with its content, and so need only sketch its position in a manner sufficient to recall that content to your memory. The focus, then, is on the functions of theology, rather than on its abstract nature or its field of data or its formal object. And those functions divide at once into two sets, according to the general law of any discipline that studies a cultural past to guide its future;[38] that is, we must hear the word, receiving it in tradition from our forefathers, and we must pass it on, taking our own stand, adapting it to our own times, and communicating it to our contemporaries and our descendants.

But each set of functions, each of the two phases of theology, divides into four, according to the dynamism of the human spirit, structured in four levels of consciousness. Thus, in the first phase, there is the assembly of the data, illustrated by a critical edition of the scriptures, or of the Fathers, or of later works of tradition. Then there is the interpretation of the data, illustrated in exegetical study of the scriptures, or of the other works which we try to understand in hearing the word from the past. Thirdly, because in these interpretations our forefathers are seen to use different languages, think in different ways, and give quite different meanings to the tradition, there is need of a history that will see the series of interpretations in a sequential pattern, and try to determine what was going forward. Fourthly, there is the critical task of evaluating the different interpretations, discovering the hidden suppositions at work in their authors, not forgetting that we ourselves are prone to understand the data within the limits of our own horizons; and thus, through the dialectic between past and present, between the classic text and our own development, between contemporaries and ourselves, we move toward the moment of decision.

But, of course, research, interpretation, history, and dialectic, the four functions I have been describing, could conceivably be carried out by an unbeliever, or at

least (as might be the case for a professor of religious studies) without involving
the theologian's personal commitment.
Theology is much more; the other half
(the real half, I am tempted to say) is an
articulation of his personal stance in four
further functions: Foundations, in which
he discovers interiorly the categories in
which he must express his religious atti-
tudes. Doctrines, in which he transposes
the doctrines of his tradition into terms
derived from religious interiority. System-
atics, the old *fides quaerens intellectum,*
theology as St. Thomas Aquinas and the
great thinkers conceived it (so the Thomist way is not abandoned, but it does become only one function among eight now).
And communications, which is not merely
preaching to the "simple faithful," but
adapting the message to all cultures, and
not just uttering the message but building
up the church and the people of God.

Such is the structure of theology. But,
because incarnate spirit has not only a
structure but its own history, the tasks
have to be done over and over, with con-

tinual feedback from the last task of communications into the first task of assembly of the data. And so theology is an ongoing spiral rather than a circle finished in some great system that will last for all time.

I have conceived Lonergan's lifework as that of creating a fundamental method and have given this subdivision of my lecture a corresponding title. But I have spoken only of method in the theological enterprise, and will continue to do so in my next section, omitting wide areas of the humanities. It is time to rectify the omission, though I propose to do so, not by spelling out the elements of method in philosophy and the sciences, as a well-proportioned and integral study would do, but simply by indicating the wider relevance of Lonergan's thought. One cannot do everything at once or even over time, so I must be content to write, as it were, a chapter title, and leave the unwritten chapter for others to complete.

The wider relevance of the eight functional specialties was most clearly affirmed by Lonergan in answering a question of Karl Rahner, whether this method is specifically theological. The answer is quite categorical and worth quoting:

> Clearly functional specialties as such are not specifically theological. Indeed, the eight specialties we have listed would be relevant to any human studies that investigated a cultural past to guide its future. Again, since the sources to be subjected to research are not specified, they could be the sacred books and traditions of any religion.[39]

The method, then, that in Lonergan's own book is applied most directly to theology, and with special reference on occasion to Roman Catholic theology, is conceived as applicable to all theology, to the study of any religion that relies on a past, and to any human studies that regard the past not merely as a source for museum pieces but as bearing on our own existential present. And Lonergan goes even further; there is a sense in which the tasks apply to science as well as to scholarship:

> . . . the functional specialties of research, interpretation, and history can be applied to the

data of any sphere of scholarly human studies. The same three specialties when conceived, not as specialties, but simply as experience, understanding, and judgment, can be applied to the data of any sphere of human living to obtain the classic principles and laws or the statistical trends of scientific human studies.[40]

The general point is perhaps clear. Law, education, the range of the human sciences, and philosophy, of course, are open to the procedure of the eight functional specialties. But I must excuse myself from pursuing their application into those fields. Lonergan's application was to theology, that is the field where I myself am most at home, and to that field I must restrict for the present my own efforts to understand and apply the method we have been studying.

IV. *Lonergan's Method as Organon*

Lonergan does not designate his work as an organon, the way Bacon did; the word does not occur anywhere in his writings, so far as I remember, to describe what he is attempting to do. But he is entirely explicit about his concern to con-

struct a method, and to distinguish that
task from the tasks of theology itself: "I
am writing not theology but method in
theology. I am concerned not with the
objects that theologians expound but with
the operations that theologians perform."[41]
When he comes to the fifth functional specialty, foundations, he contrasts it with
traditional fundamental theology; that was
a part of theology, for it was a set of doctrines: on the true religion, on the divine
legate who is Christ, etc. "In contrast,
foundations present, not doctrines, but the
horizon within which the meaning of doctrines can be apprehended."[42] Even when
he lists the categories of a methodical
theology, he insists: ". . . the task of a
methodologist is to sketch the derivation
of such categories, but it is up to the theologian working in the fifth functional
specialty to determine in detail what the
general and special categories are to be."[43]
Lonergan's method, then, can be distin-
guished from theology, as logic is dis-
tinguished from philosophy, and scientific
method from science itself and its findings.

In other words it can be conceived as an organon in the way the Aristotelians and Bacon understood the term.

Now I am not going to argue for the substitution, throughout Lonergan's writings, of the word "organon" for the word "method." But it is worth asking whether the familiarity of the latter word is not responsible for too simple a view of what Lonergan is about and what tasks he has set for us. Certainly, if one consults the bibliographies of current literature (lists of doctoral dissertations are a good index here), one will find literally thousands of entries under the heading, method. Mostly they deal with methods of teaching, methods of counseling, and the like, but sometimes (such is the omnivorous range of doctoral candidates) they may deal with such quite particular specializations as methods of shot-putting. And the notion can readily form that Lonergan's method is another in such a series, despite his careful definition in the first chapter of the book *Method in Theology*.

If so, it may be helpful to conceive his

work and contribution more specifically as an organon. For, first of all, "organon" in itself conveys a better idea of what is intended. The root meaning of method is that of following a way, but the root meaning of organon is that of a functioning part of a living whole; it conveys a notion, then, of something more substantive than a method. Further, a way is external to the traveler; an organon is part of his very being and nature. And so a way is traveled and left behind; but an organon functions today, and remains to function likewise tomorrow. Ways are many, sometimes optional, and always derivative from a guiding intelligence; an organon is unique, lies behind all its functioning, is versatile and adaptable to varying situations. Hence it is that one will speak of many methods: mathematical, empirical, philosophical, and theological; but one will speak of a single organon that functions in any or all of these methods. There is reason, then, on grounds of basic meaning, to affirm that "organon" does more justice to the lifework of Lonergan than does "method,"

though I would not claim that all the
points I have listed can be transferred
from the root meaning to the metaphorical.
But, second and more important, there is
reason on historical grounds to conceive
Lonergan's work as we have done. For the
Aristotelian and Baconian efforts in this
direction have provided models, have es-
tablished precedents, and have given our
term a meaning in philosophical writing
and a place in the history of philosophical
thinking, that make it somewhat more difficult now to misunderstand what a thinker
is about when he would offer the world a
new organon and would communicate his
idea on what constitutes it.

Finally, while appreciating the advan-
tage of conceiving Lonergan's work in a
series with that of Aristotle and Bacon, we
should take full notice of the contrast between Lonergan's idea and those of the
logical Aristotle and the empirical Bacon.
Thus, logic for Lonergan is derivative from
the dynamism of incarnate spirit: "Upon
the normative exigences of the pure desire
[to know] rests the validity of all logics

and all methods,"[44] and this is spelled out for the principles of identity, contradiction, and excluded middle.[45] But the same remark can be made about the procedures of empirical method. Chapter Two of *Insight* "moved not forward and outward to conclusions about objects but rather backward and inward to the subject's anticipations of insights that have not occurred and to the methodical exploitation of such anticipations. In that inward movement the reader can foresee the direction in which the whole work will advance. . . . Our goal is the concrete, individual, existing subject . . . the restless dynamism of human understanding."[46]

So Lonergan's own work aims far beyond the rules of logic or the procedures of empirical method. He described his book *Insight* as an "essay in aid of a personal appropriation of one's own rational self-consciousness,"[47] and that self-appropriation would function as "*a fixed base, an invariant pattern, opening upon all further developments of understanding.*"[48] *Method* extends the base: "For the first chapter . . . sets forth what they [the readers] can discover in themselves as the dynamic structure of their own cognitional and moral being. . . . Moreover, subsequent chapters are in the main prolongations of the first."[49] Again, "There is then a rock on which one can build. . . . The rock . . . is the subject in his conscious, unobjectified attentiveness, intelligence, reasonableness, responsibility."[50] To this must be added the footnote Lonergan inserts: "It will become evident in Chapter Four that the more important part of the rock has not yet been uncovered,"[51] namely, the gift of God's love effecting our religious conversion and enabling us to do theology as believers and not mere observers, to add the four functions of the second phase of theology to those of the first phase.[52] And so the whole complex organon is based on the interiority of incarnate spirit, with its gifts of nature and of grace.

To see Lonergan's work as an organon, therefore, and to see how far this *organum novissimum*[53] goes beyond the original *Organon* of Aristotelian logic and the *Novum*

Organum of Bacon's experimental science, gives us a new appreciation of his contribution to the history of ideas. I say this with the sincere wish to pay full tribute to the work of those earlier thinkers. Genius is not to be measured against the achievements of later, but against those of preceding centuries. By that measure the position in history of Aristotle and Bacon is assured—not that it depends, in any case, solely on the logic of the one or the empirical procedures of the other. By that measure too we may expect that Lonergan's position in history will be safe in the twenty-fifth century when others have gone far beyond him; may his critics then give him all the credit we wish to give here to Aristotle and Bacon.

But we are not measuring genius; we are comparing achievements, and in particular the programmatic value for future progress of instruments of incarnate spirit. And then I think we have to recognize how limited are the uses of logic for the restless and world-creating dynamism of human spirit, and how limited is the value of the observations and experiments of empirical science, even for empirical science itself, and still more for exploring the great spaces of the inner world, the domains of the human, philosophical, and theological sciences. Matthew Arnold said of Sophocles, in a much-quoted statement, that he saw life steadily and saw it whole. A parallel statement must be made of the creator of that instrument of human spirit we have in *Insight* and *Method:* he saw, or came to see in growing clarity, the complex resources of incarnate spirit, and he saw them in the whole vast range of their restless dynamism.

Concluding Remarks

My effort has been to see Fr. Lonergan's lifework as a whole, or at least to arrive at such an approximation as is possible now, while the work goes on, of an overall view, of an intelligible unity in the materials at hand. Possibly such an effort on my part will be seen as misguided in principle, unity in these matters being regarded as a chimera. It is true, so I am

told, that the old classical unities for a
work of art have broken down; maybe they
were never meant anyway to yield more
than ideal types. As for history, Aristotle
would not, I suppose, attempt a unity even
to that limited extent; and later thinkers
who have tried to encompass history in a
single pattern have come under severe
criticism, just as biographers who would
reconstruct a life in some more or less intelligible unity are bound to suffer from
the critics. But I have not been doing a
biography; I have simply been trying to
contribute to that part of it which is an
intellectual history, a much more limited
project. And, though there are dialectical
sequences as well as genetic that would
have to be taken into account in a full
story, still we are allowed to suppose,
when dealing with a thinker of Lonergan's
stature, that there is something approaching a unity in the unfolding sequence of
his intellectual odyssey.

It is another question than one of principle whether the particular pattern I have
sketched as unifying principle is the best,

or even satisfactory. The preliminary test of such a principle is no doubt its ability to integrate a maximum of the materials into the pattern in some way or other: as instrumental, complementary, genetic, dialectical, or whatever. For example, I would integrate Lonergan's work in actual theology (on grace, Christ, providence, Trinity, etc.) by seeing it as the arena in which he worked out his method and brought it by successive steps to something approaching definitive form. Others might reverse the direction, and see the method as subordinate to the theology, or as tangential, or in some other way. Or they might wish to follow another principle altogether, seeing his intellectual history as structured by the steps in his appropriation of the dynamism of incarnate spirit: cognitional theory, values, opening to the interpersonal, and so on. Everyone is, of course, welcome to try his own hand at structuring the materials. But I would point out that the project is not just a curious intellectual exercise. Ideas have consequences, and the way we see Loner-

gan's contribution as a whole will determine the way we locate him in history, the
challenge we find him presenting to us,
and so the response we make to that
challenge.

For one thing, on the view I have pre-
sented, the history in which we will locate
him is not the history of the past; that also
is a task that must sometime be under-
taken, but the really significant history is
that of the future—which means leaving the
job to later generations. For a successful
instrument is better known by its further
history than by its earlier inchoative steps.
Who knows or cares much about the prior
history of the wheel or the prior history
of the alphabet? It is what was done sub-
sequently through the use of the wheel,
through the use of the alphabet, that cap-
tures our imagination. The impact of an
instrument of mind, to return to Bacon's
term, is not likely to be as palpable and
easy to trace as the impact of the wheel.
Still it is there. You can measure the influence of Aristotelian logic sixteen centuries later in the thinking of St. Thomas

Aquinas. Not that you will find syllogisms in proper form in St. Thomas; you may read a long time before you find a syllogism at all. But you will certainly read a long time before you find a fault in logic by Aristotelian standards—the great work of the *Organon* had entered the very stuff and texture of the mind and thinking of Aquinas.[54] In a similar way, if Jaspers is right in asserting the almost inconceivable magnitude of the transition we are experiencing, if I am right in seeing in Lonergan's method an instrument for the new human science which that transition will necessitate, an instrument that is apt, powerful, versatile, far-ranging, an instrument *par excellence* for the time and its need, then the history that belongs to the creator of that instrument lies in the future. So it is appropriate to speak of the Lonergan enterprise. David Tracy has written of the Lonergan achievement, and quite rightly, for without the achievement there would be no enterprise for us to undertake; but the enterprise will in the long run dwarf the achievement.

A second consequence, and it is hardly more than a specification of the first, is that the theology envisaged by Lonergan's method remains to be written—the whole of it, complete and entire. And how much of philosophy and the human sciences likewise remains to be written I can hardly conjecture. I do not mean that we will jettison the nineteen hundred and twenty-nine years of thinking since St. Paul wrote his First Letter to the Thessalonians. But it will have to be reoriented in the steps of research, interpretation, and history, submitted to criticism and allowed to challenge us in dialectic, provided with its foundations in interiority, and restated in doctrines for our times, before we can do theology again in the manner of St. Thomas Aquinas.

A third consequence simply instantiates that need by a confession of the psychological difficulty, amounting to an impossibility, which students of Lonergan experience in taking a stand on current theological questions. Lonergan himself has been almost completely silent for fifteen years

on the issues that rage around us, and this
is sometimes adduced as a datum to lower
our estimate of his importance for the
times. The datum is hardly to be disputed,
but it is to be interpreted in exactly the
contrary sense: It is an index of the stature
of his thinking and the magnitude of the
enterprise he has set afoot. Those of us
who have been deeply affected by his work
realize that vividly and painfully. To take
a minor instance, I find myself almost at a
loss when asked for my theological views
on current questions: the status of women
in the church, the magisterium, the meaning of religious life, original sin, ministry,
infallibility, and the rest. I can only remain
at one remove from an answer and detail
the necessary steps to take in order to arrive at a solution. We would need a history
of the thinking of the church in the past,
a history of course based on well-assem-
bled data, but one especially that shows
us the sequence of interpretations the data
have received, and the variety of options
the thinking of the past has offered; then
we would need to reduce those options to

their sources in the horizons of the particular thinkers or groups or cultures involved,
to determine our own horizons and analyze
our own situation, to see what transposi-
tions could and should be made from the
past into the present, and so on in the
familiar steps of the functional specialties.
But it is quite impossible to attack such
questions methodically and do it alone.
One can putter about at bits of history
where one by long reading has gleaned
some sense from the scholars of what was
going forward; but one cannot do dialectic
alone, without dialectic foundations will
not be laid securely, and without foundations we have no appropriate statement of
doctrines for our times. Collaboration then
is needed, and the collaboration has to be
institutionalized on the grand scale. Mean-
while there is a sense in which we are re-
duced to silence on the great questions.[55]

But life cannot mark time in this "mean-
while," or take "time out" from activity;
life goes on. Life needs thinking; thinking
in religious questions becomes some kind
of theology; and none of this can wait till

Jaspers' new era has arrived, till some
method has been found, Lonergan's or another, to make us feel at home in our new
world. I sometimes reflect what a disaster
it would be if all theologians were as
deeply infected by the Lonergan enterprise as I am; there would be a great
silence in the theological universe, longer
by far, I am afraid, than the half-hour in
heaven of which the Apocalypse speaks
(though we would hope for a happier
sequel). Fortunately, no doubt providen-
tially, there are multitudes of theologians
not so infected. Consequently, the work
goes on; far from silence in the theological
universe, we experience a continual up-
roar. What is of some importance, from
the methodical viewpoint I have adopted,
is to categorize this ongoing work. For
some observers and participants, of course,
it may be the emergence of the very theology we need. They may be right (who
would be so dogmatic as to deny it?) and,
if they are, more power to those who are
creating this theology. But one of the
greatest of them refers to his own work as

that of a dilettante.[56] No one here, I hope,
will accept Rahner's application of this
term to his own work, but the very esteem
in which we hold him will lead us to take
seriously his underlying analysis of the
present situation, and to agree with him
on the importance of the question he is
trying to answer, whether there is a new
genus litterarium of theological work today, and, if so, how to characterize it.[57]
Personally, I would think rather of an interim theology, one that does what is possible at the moment to tide us over difficult times, and I would do so on the
analogy of patristic theology before St.
Augustine more or less got it all together,
at least for the West, or on the analogy of
early scholastic theology before St. Thomas
Aquinas arrived on the scene. We do not
expect that there will ever again be an
Augustine or an Aquinas (and if there
were, he or she would not be another
Augustine or an Aquinas, as Aquinas was
not just another Augustine), but we do
hope for a company of theologians, working with that degree of community in un-

derstanding, judgment, and commitment,
which is necessary for collaboration, who
would be the collective Augustine or
Aquinas of the future.

Let me close with a word of personal
appreciation for what I regard as a lifetime of self-sacrificing dedication to a single great idea at one remove from its consequences, the dedication of one who sows
and will not live to reap. Adolf Harnack
has spoken of the "self-sacrificing deeds"
and "the surrender of life itself" that form
"the turning-point in every great advance
in history." His example was Martin
Luther: "Did Luther in the monastery
strive only for himself?—was it not for us
all that he inwardly bled . . .?"[58] My example, of course, is Bernard Lonergan, whose
whole life has been one of renouncement
of the immediate small gain for the sake
of the great harvest of the future.[59]

We should be clear on the degree of
sacrifice involved in such a decision: To
withdraw from the hunt when there is
quarry immediately before one, to post-
pone the pursuit while giving oneself to

the forging of a new and vastly superior instrument, to be willing, and eventually to determine, to spend one's entire life at that task (hoping that the long-term benefits will make it worthwhile, but knowing with certainty that one will not see the full harvest and realizing that at best one's efforts will be appreciated only by a small band of attentive readers and students), to live the long years perseveringly, hopefully, unwaveringly, in the labor of creating an adequate organon of incarnate spirit—that withdrawal, renouncement, willingness, decision, and perseverance is not the act of a drifter or a self-seeker. It is an act of notable self-transcendence, one that we who share Fr. Lonergan's estimate of the momentousness of our times and of the magnitude of the task before us, should be able to appreciate, one we should allow to challenge us to contribute our own share of sacrifice and labor toward a task that promises so much for the whole people of God.[60]

FOOTNOTES

1. *Philosophy and the World: Selected Essays and Lectures* (Chicago: Henry Regnery Company, 1963), p. 22.

2. I. Bertoni, "Organo," *Enciclopedia Filosofica*, 4 vols. (Venice/Rome: Istituto per la collaborazione culturale, 1957), 3: cols. 1075-76. I have not been able to find a detailed study of the history of this idea but, as I have experienced before, the Italian encyclopedias are invaluable in supplying something for the deficiency.

3. W. A. De Pater, *Les Topiques d'Aristote et la dialectique platonicienne: Méthodologie de la définition* (Fribourg: Editions St. Paul [Thomistische Studien X] 1965), p. 129; J. M. Le Blond, *Logique et méthode chez Aristote: Etude sur la recherche des principes dans la Physique Aristotélicenne* (Paris: J. Vrin, 1939), p. 38.

4. W. D. Ross, *Aristotle*, 2nd ed. (London: Methuen & Co., 1930), p. 20.

5. Frederick Copleston, *A History of Philosophy*, 9 vols. (London: Burns, Oates, and Washbourne, 1946-   ), 1:426-27.

6. Ross, *Aristotle*, p. 20.

7. John Leofric Stocks, *Aristotelianism* (London: G. G. Harrap & Co., undated), pp. 149-50, 154.

8. James Collins, *A History of Modern European Philosophy* (Milwaukee: Bruce Pub. Co., 1954), p. 57. It was simpler to turn to Collins for a succinct statement on this point than to reduce the prolixity of Bacon himself; for a sample of the latter, see Francis Bacon, *Essays, Advancement of Learning, New Atlantis, and Other Pieces,* selected and edited by Richard Foster Jones (New York: Odyssey Press, 1937), p. 202: "This kind of degenerate learning did chiefly reign amongst the schoolmen, who having sharp and strong wits and abundance of leisure and small variety

of reading, but their wits being shut up in the cells of a few authors (chiefly Aristotle their dictator) as their persons were shut up in the cells of monasteries and colleges, and knowing little history, either of nature or time, did out of no great quantity of matter and infinite agitation of wit spin out unto us those laborious webs of learning which are extant in their books." For more compact statements, see Aphorisms xi-xiv, ibid., p. 274.

9. Bacon, *Essays*, pp. 239-40.

10. Collins, *A History of Modern European Philosophy*, p. 58.

11. Bacon, *Essays*, pp. 237, 266. We remember that Kant, bent on a similar project, took some lines from the Preface of the *Magna Instauratio* as a motto for his *Critique of Pure Reason* (p. 4 of Norman Kemp Smith's edition of the *Critique* [New York: Dutton, 1950]).

12. Bacon, *Essays*, p. 268.

13. Ibid., p. 272.

14. Ibid., Aphorisms, no. cxiii, p. 323.

15. Ibid., no. cxvi, p. 325.

16. R. F. Jones, "The Bacon of the Seventeenth Century," *Essential Articles for the Study of Francis Bacon*, ed. Brian Vickers (Hamden, Conn.: Archon Books, 1968) pp. 3-27; see p. 21.

17. V. K. Whitaker, "Francis Bacon's Intellectual Milieu," ibid., pp. 28-49; see p. 39.

18. Ibid., p. 41.

19. *A Second Collection: Papers by Bernard J. F. Lonergan, S.J.*, ed. W. F. J. Ryan and B. J. Tyrrell (London: Darton, Longman and Todd, 1974, p. 67 (in "Theology in Its New Context").

20. Ibid., p. 161 (in "The Future of Christianity").

21. Bacon, *Essays*, pp. 239-40.

22. "St. Thomas' Thought on *Gratia Operans*," *Theological Studies* 2 (1941): 289-324; 3 (1942): 69-88;

375-402; 533-78. Reprinted in book form, *Grace and Freedom: Operative Grace in the Thought of St. Thomas Aquinas,* ed. J. Patout Burns (London: Darton, Longman, and Todd: New York, Herder and Herder, 1971).

23. Page 4 of the original thesis, *Gratia Operans: A Study of the Speculative Development in the Writings of St. Thomas of Aquin.* For the Doctorate in Sacred Theology, Rome, Gregorian University, 1940.

24. Ibid., p. 10 (a minor misprint in the typescript has been corrected).

25. Ibid., p. 5.

26. Ibid., p. 34; and see pp. 33-34.

27. "The Concept of *Verbum* in the Writings of St. Thomas Aquinas," *Theological Studies* 7 (1946): 349-92; 8 (1947): 35-79; 404-44; 10 (1949): 3-40; 359-93. Reprinted in book form, *Verbum: Word and Idea in Aquinas,* ed. David B. Burrell (Notre Dame, Ind.: University of Notre Dame Press, 1967).

28. Bernard J. F. Lonergan, *Insight: A Study of Human Understanding* (London: Longmans, Green and Co., 1957; 4th ed., San Francisco: Harper and Row, 1978).

29. "Theology and Understanding," *Gregorianum* 35 (1954): 630-48; reprinted as ch. 8 in *Collection: Papers by Bernard Lonergan, S.J.,* ed. F. E. Crowe (New York: Herder and Herder, 1967), pp. 121-41.

30. Lonergan, *Collection,* p. 135.

31. Lonergan, *Divinarum personarum conceptio analogica* (Rome: Pontificia Universitas Gregoriana, 1957)—this, in revised form, became vol. 2 of *De Deo Trino* (Rome: Pontificia Universitas Gregoriana, 1964); *De Deo Trino: Pars analytica* (Rome: Pontificia Universitas Gregoriana, 1961)—this, again in revised form, became vol 1 of *De Deo Trino* (Rome, 1964).

32. This pair of terms has a long history, documented to some extent by Henry Guerlac, "Newton and the

Method of Analysis," *Dictionary of the History of Ideas* ed. Philip P. Wiener (New York: Charles Scribner's Sons, 1973), 3: 378-91 (the *Dictionary* has no article under either Analysis or Synthesis). Lonergan's use of the term derives from Aristotle and Aquinas (see *Verbum: Word and Idea in Aquinas*, and references in the Index under "Via").

33. Lonergan, *Collection*, p. 133.

34. Lonergan, *Divinarum personarum conceptio analogica* (Rome, 1957). But my text makes its point a little too sharply. The historical way is not an afterthought; sect. 4, pp. 20-23, is entitled, "De triplici motu quo ad finem procedatur"; sect. 5, pp. 23-28, "Comparantur motus analyticus et syntheticus"; and sect. 6, pp. 28-34, "Tertii et historici motus additur consideratio." It is true, however, that the analytic-synthetic pair are complementary to one another and form a unit if one prescinds from history; see p. 12 of *De intellectu et methodo* (student notes of a course given by Lonergan at the Gregorian University, 1959): "Si praetermittitur historia, uterque ordo est splendidus; at historia exsistit . . . ."

35. Lonergan, *Collection,* p. 141; see the whole section, pp. 134-41.

36. Lonergan, *Method in Theology* (London: Darton, Longman and Todd, 1972).

37. And on the use we make of it, for there is no guarantee that his work will not lie fallow forever due to reader neglect; the spontaneities of human consciousness will surely remain and be operative, but they will not lead infallibly to their own accurate objectification, much less to their implementation in a corresponding method.

38. "Bernard Lonergan Responds," *Foundations of Theology,* ed. Philip McShane (Dublin and London: Gill and Macmillan, 1971); see p. 233.

39. Ibid., p. 233.

40. Lonergan, *Method,* pp. 364-65. Lonergan suggests a

convention for the use of "science" and "scholarship," ibid., pp. 233-34; see also p. 180. On the relation of his "generalized empirical method" and "the particular methods adapted to the needs and opportunities of particular fields," he has a useful section in his article, "The Ongoing Genesis of Methods," *Studies in Religion* 6 (1976-77): 341-55; see pp. 344-45.

41. Lonergan, *Method,* p. xii.

42. Ibid., p. 131.

43. Ibid., p. 291; see also pp. 149, 253-54, 282, 297-98, 312, 323-24, and 355, for further allusions to the distinction between theology and methodology.

44. Lonergan, *Insight,* p. 380.

45. Ibid., p. 381; see also p. 304. Likewise *Verbum,* pp. 33-34; and *A Second Collection,* p. 76 (in "The Subject").

46. Lonergan, *Insight,* pp. 68-69.

47. Ibid., p. 748.

48. Ibid., p. xxviii.

49. Lonergan, *Method,* p. xii.

50. Ibid., pp. 19-20.

51. Ibid., p. 19.

52. Ibid., pp. 105-107, 130-32.

53. I avoid the term, Tertium Organum. Partly on general grounds, because the history of the idea has been but sketched, Bertoni's article (see n. 2 above) being almost unique. Partly for the particular reason that P. D. Ouspensky has preempted the term, and this in direct relation to the first and second *organa* of Aristotle and Bacon; see his *Tertium Organum. A Key to the Enigmas of the World* (New York: Vintage Books, 1970, paperback edition), p. 236. Some may feel that, after more than sixty years during which this rather mystical work has failed to secure attention, we might safely ignore it. But, if I am to be true to my own principles in such matters, I must leave that kind of judgment and evaluation to others. —A much more

interesting question: For what precisely are we claiming the term, organon? Is it (1) the dynamism itself of incarnate spirit, or (2) its objectification in the transcendental precepts, or (3) the articulation of a method according to the structure of the precepts? Not (1), I would say, for that is operative independently of the work of any thinker; and more properly (2) than (3) for the basic objectification remains the same instrument in a variety of methods. And a still further question: the relation of "canons" to "organon" and "method," a question to be researched in history and in Lonergan himself.

54. Is something analogous to be said about Bacon's influence? It is not for me to answer that question, with the experts divided. See, for the debit side of the ledger, the highly critical essay of Morris R. Cohen, "Bacon and the Inductive Method," pp. 99-106 in his book, *Studies in Philosophy and Science* (New York: H. Holt, 1949). Mary Hesse summarizes some merits and demerits of Bacon in "Francis Bacon's Philosophy of Science," pp. 114-39 in the Vickers volume (see n. 16 above); see p. 138 of her article. Recall also the remark of R. F. Jones (quoted on p. 22 of my text) that Bacon's "influence on the scientific movement was general rather than specific."

55. May I illustrate the point still further from my own experience. Over twenty years ago I began to construct for my students a little "treatise" on the word of God; it came to consist of two parts, one more positive and historical (analytic) and one more speculative and systematic (synthetic). My students, as is the way of students, were much more drawn by the second part than by the first, and when my book, *Theology of the Christian Word: A Study in History* (New York: Paulist Press, 1978) finally came out last year, disappointment was expressed that I had included nothing of the speculative part of the earlier notes. But the explanation is simply that we are nowhere near the point where we can do that task of theology properly. This does not prevent me from

doing my own interim theology on occasion and according to need; for example, one cannot pray in the
Ignatian manner without coming to some understanding of the mind and heart of Christ, and I have twice
returned to that question, which we are far from
ready as yet to handle methodically.

56. Karl Rahner, "Einfache Klarstellung zum eigenen
Werk," *Schriften zur Theologie* 12 (Zürich: Benziger,
1975): 599-604. This is not the sort of evaluation
made on his own work by Thomas Aquinas in his last
year (a thing of "straw"), for that remark is judged
to result from a comparison of achieved with mys-
tically given knowledge. Nor is it a casual and unre-
flected statement, for it is the revised form of a piece
Rahner had written five years earlier (ibid., p. 599).
Further, Rahner returns to it three years later; see
John Coulson, "In the presence of Newman," *The
Tablet* (London), Sept. 23, 1978, pp. 928-29, and
his account of Rahner's participation in a recent Newman congress. We have to realize that Rahner is
grappling with a real question, and doing so with his
habitual profundity. I think we can accept this without accepting Rahner's evaluation of his own work,
though naturally, in the "growing pains" of the
church, others will find occasion here to belittle that
work; see A. Zürich, "Carlo Rahner nega di essere
filosofo e si autoqualifica dilettante in teologia," *Divus
Thomas* 82 (1979): 19-28.

57. On the general relation between the work of Rahner
and Lonergan, let me state my opinion, since the
comparison is so often made, that the project can be
profitable but there are real pitfalls to avoid. For the
Lonergan term of the comparison, one should not
take his Latin theology without a clear idea of its
status in his development: it has still to be put
through the crucible of his own method to see what
can be salvaged; as for the theology that does result
from that method, it has not been written, so no comparison is possible. There are scattered elements of
theology in Lonergan's recent writings which might

be brought into profitable comparison with the corresponding but more elaborately worked out ideas of Rahner; but I wonder if the fully legitimate and most promising field of comparative study is not Rahner's *Spirit in the World* and *Hearers of the Word* on one side, and Lonergan's *Insight* and *Method* on the other.

58. Adolf Harnack, *What is Christianity?* 3rd ed. (London: Williams and Norgate; New York: G. P. Putnam's Sons, 1904), pp. 161-62.

59. For a sample of what "might have been" in the area of such immediate gains, I suggest "Finality, Love, Marriage" (*Collection*, pp. 16-53). Published in 1943. it reveals the potentiality that might have found realization in scores of similar efforts to deepen our theology of current problems, had not the author determined on another use of his allotted time and energies.

60. This lecture in somewhat different form was given in various Australian cities during April and May of 1979. In October of the same year it became the first in a three-part series at Gonzaga University, Spokane, known as the St. Michael's Lectures; the series is to be published under the title, *The Lonergan Enterprise*. My warm thanks are due to the organizers of both the Australian and the Gonzaga University series, and to the audiences who attended the delivery of the lecture and made it such a pleasant learning experience for me.

The Pere Marquette Theology Lectures

1969: "The Authority for Authority,"
by Quentin Quesnell
Professor of Theology at
Marquette University

1970: "Mystery and Truth,"
by John Macquarrie
Professor of Theology at
Union Theology Seminary, New York

1971: "Doctrinal Pluralism,"
by Bernard Lonergan, S.J.
Professor of Theology at
Regis College, Ontario

1972: "Infallibility,"
by George A. Lindbeck
Professor of Theology at
Yale University

1973: "Ambiguity in Moral Choice,"
by Richard A. McCormick, S.J.
Professor of Moral Theology at
Bellarmine School of Theology

1974: "Church Membership as a Catholic
and Ecumenical Problem,"
by Avery Dulles, S.J.
Professor of Theology at
Woodstock College

1975: "The Contributions of Theology to
Medical Ethics,"
by James Gustafson
University Professor of Theological Ethics at
University of Chicago

1976: "Religious Values in an Age of Violence,"
by Rabbi Marc Tanenbaum
Director of National Interreligious Affairs
American Jewish Committee, New York City

1977: "Truth Beyond Relativism: Karl Mannheim's
Sociology of Knowledge,"
by Gregory Baum
Professor of Theology and Religious Studies at
St. Michael's College

1978: "A Theology of 'Uncreated Energies' "
by George A. Maloney, S.J.
Professor of Theology
John XXIII Center For Eastern Christian Studies
Fordham University

1980: "Method in Theology: An Organon For
Our Time"
by Frederick E. Crowe, S.J.
Research Professor in Theology
Regis College, Toronto

Copies of this lecture and the others in the series are obtainable from:

Marquette University Press
Marquette University
Milwaukee, Wisconsin 53233
USA